THE JAGUAR PEOPLE

NORTHWATER

CONSTANTINE ISSIGHOS

Copyright 2012 © Constantine Issighos. Published in Canada. Printed in U.S.A. No part of this book may be reproduced or transmitted in any form or by any means, electronic or mechanical, including photocopying, recording, and/or by any information storage and retrieval system except by a reviewer who may quote brief passages in a review to be printed in a magazine, newspaper, or on the web without written permission in writing from the author/publisher. For information, please contact www.awaqkunabooks.com

NorthWater is an imprint of Awaqkuna Books Inc.

Vol. 14 of THE AMAZON EXPLORATION SERIES:

THE JAGUAR PEOPLE

Library and Archives Canada

ISBN 978-0-9878601-3-2

Library and Archives Canada Cataloguing in Publication

ATTENTION CHILDRENS ASSOCIATIONS, BOOK STORES, PUBLIC OR PRIVATE LIBRARIES: quantity discounts are available on bulk purchases of this book series.

THE AMAZON EXPLORATION SERIES

Children's Books
by
Constantine Issighos

1. Upper Amazon Voyage by River Boat
2. The People of the River
3. The Children of the River
4. Amazon's Nature of Things
5. Echoes of Nature: a Beautiful Wild Habitat
6. The Amazon Rainforest
7. Amazonian Sisterhood
8. Amazon River Wolves
9. Amazonian Landscapes and Sunsets
10. Amazonian Canopy: the Roof of the World's Rainforest
11. Amazonian Tribes: a World of Difference
12. Birds, Flowers and Butterflies of the Amazon
13. The Great Wonders of the Amazon
14. The Jaguar People
15. The Fresh Water Giants
16. The Call of the Shaman
17. Indigenous Families: Life in Harmony with Nature
18. Amazon in Peril
19. Giant Tarantulas and Centipedes
20. The Amazon Ethno-Botanical Garden
21. The Real Amazon Tribal Warriors

The Mayoranas

Long ago, before the invention of agriculture and husbandry, the entire human race survived as fishermen and hunters. Today, only a handful of Amazonian tribes practice this ancient way of life. Observing and photographing such Amazonian tribes is more than a foreigner's curiosity; it is a glimpse into the mist of human history, giving us a chance to see how our ancestors lived.

Historical evidence shows that where a human population settled, the physical and cultural characteristics of that community were developed based on the environmental conditions to which it had to adapt. They identified with the peculiarities of their terrain and adopted mannerisms that resembled the metaphorical aspects of that environment. Thus, survival methods and people's cultural development were both rooted in the conditions of the people's physical surroundings.

One clearly sees evidence of both principles with the Mayoranas tribe—better known as the "cat people." Their method of survival is based on the Amazonian jungle conditions; they survive by hunting and fishing. They are called the "cat people" due to the ornamental "jaguar-whiskers" their members place in their noses. The cultural ornament is made of the ribs of palm leaves and placed in their noses to represent the whiskers of the jaguar. Through the wearing of facial ornaments they pay a mystical homage to the jaguar and its incredible hunting skills.

This revered jaguar is the largest land carnivore in most of its range. This powerful yet furtive predator has captured the Mayoranas' imagination since time immemorial. In their cultural inner-workings they believe that their shaman—medicine doctor—can transform himself into a jaguar. The jaguar of the Amazon basin has a powerful compact body that exudes strength; it is built for stealth and sudden capture, a hunting technique that it is adopted by the Mayoranas hunters.

Like the jaguar, the Mayoranas occupy a variety of habitats: from short dry forest to a combination of savannah and forest, to deep primary and secondary rainforest. Both the jaguar and the Mayoranas hunters have prey which includes peccaries, rodents--pica, agouti, and capybara--armadillos and deer.

Jaguars have long whiskers and a yellowish coat with a pattern of black spots called rosettes, essentially rings with dots within. For the Mayoranas hunters, the cat's spotted coat represents the night sky and they see its shiny, reflective eyes as proof of its connection to the spiritual world.

The Mayoranas men are also incredible hunters. They use bows and arrows as well as the blowgun which shoots tiny poisonous darts through a 10-foot long tube. The hunter first dips the tip of the dart into a powerful poison, and when the tip hits the target, the poison paralyzes the prey's nervous system. The Mayoranas hunters are so accurate with their blowgun that they are known for being able to kill a hummingbird in flight up to 100 feet away. The Mayoranas use their bows and arrows for both hunting in the jungle and catching fish in shallow river waters. The jaguar catches fish with its powerful claws. The ability to catch fish is crucial to the survival of both the jaguar and the Mayoranas.

For the Mayoranas men, paying homage to the jaguar is embedded with cultural meanings connecting human and non-human, honouring wild nature and what it has to offer. In their cosmos, the Amazon rainforest is simultaneously wild and sacred, a food source and a cultural script.

In the Mayoranas culture, there is a strong association between the jaguar and the spiritual world of shamanism. It is very difficult for me to describe the "shaman-jaguar complex" found among the "jaguar-people" of the Mayoranas because I am not of their culture. The central characteristic of the complex, however, is the association of shamans share the jaguars and the belief that the shamans have the power to be transformed into jaguars.

The jaguar is a solitary animal, a quintessentially wild and dangerous hunter. All hunters are extremely good at imitating the jaguar, and the shaman's transformation into jaguar is for their protection. There is a direct association between the Mayoranas' mysticism and hunting. It is an integral part of the co-existence of Mayoranas peoples with their natural environment.

Today, this ancient belief is found in limited areas of the Amazon Basin. Is there a need for western men to recognize our animal selves—as the Mayoranas indigenous people do—animal selves that mirror who we are back to us, in order to see who we once were?

The Piraha

Another unique group are the Piraha, an indigenous hunter-gatherer tribe of the Brazilian Amazon. I was very interested in learning as much as possible about them. They live on the riverbanks of the Maici River. They hunt by using bows and arrows—and, like the jaguar—they seek their prey in a wide range of hunting territory. While there are many reclusive tribes in Brazil, the Piraha are the most isolated and have little to no outside contact with settlers. They have a trekking lifestyle, hunting for various animals in the rainforest. Monkey is a primary source of food. Interestingly, the Piraha tribe keep the fire embers burning so they can simply start a fire when they arrive at their destination.

Their uniqueness lies with the fact that the Piraha live a life and have a culture that remains in a primitive "state of nature." The state of nature is a condition in which every man is for himself; there is no leadership power structure to keep them all in awe. In the Piraha tribe there doesn't appear to be any clear-cut leadership hierarchy that unites and directs the common goals of the tribe. Within their state of nature, every Piraha man has the natural right to preserve his own life in a solitary manner.

Theirs is a present-time living culture that does not go beyond their "here and now." Translation: their daily concern is solely with matters that fall within their direct personal experience. They deal with no past or future matters, thus they have no communal history beyond living memory, no ancestor relations any more distant than their present biological ones.

The indigenous Piraha have inhabited their hunting-fishing grounds (once considered "empty") for thousands of years living in harmony with the ecosystem. It is exciting to see that such people living in a raw state of nature still exist. In this state of nature they only consume or utilize whatever nature provides for them. They produce no food of their own making nor do they preserve their own immediate environment. Their tool-making knowledge relates specifically to their bows and arrows used for fishing and hunting.

Like the jaguar, the Piraha hunters have no regular sleeping habits. They sleep during the day or night in short naps of up to two hours. Nor do they eat regularly—not because of lack of food—but to become tougher.

They live without technology; they use no monetary system but they trade their catch with other tribes in the vicinity. They have no counting system; their language does not include words for precise numbers, and they seem incapable of learning the meaning of numeracy.

Their artwork appears to be almost non-existent. Whatever form of artwork is present is mostly necklaces and drawn stick-figures used primarily to ward off evil spirits. They appear to not have an extensive mystical fiction or mythology.

I chose to call the Piraha "The Jaguar People" as an honorary title—due to their raw predatory and solitary lifestyle—just as the jaguar itself.

The Ashanikas

The third group that I have chosen to call the "Jaguar People" are the Ashanikas tribe who live in the watersheds of the Andean range. In demographic terms, the Ashanikas are the largest indigenous population in the Peruvian Amazon basin—their numbers vary from 35,000 to 50,000. In Brazil the Ashanikas are found in the Tierra Indegena—all located in the upper Jurui region. These people originated in Peru and began their migration in the 19th century. Local historical information is vague and provides little information about the migration of the Ashanikas into Brazilian territory.

The principle activity carried out by the Ashanikas until the 1970s was the hunting of wild animals in exchange for imported goods. They supplied live animals, meat and skins which were highly valued in the Amazonian and non-indigenous markets. Trade was intensified in the 1980s to include logging of hardwood trees located in the Ashanikas territory. This had disastrous consequences for the environment and the indigenous population, profoundly affecting the social organization and cultural characteristics of the Ashanikas of the Amazon.

It was the dreadful environmental and social destruction that led to the organization of the Ashanikas community—and to the union of the tribe—in its struggle for its rights. Their effort continues to this day.

What distinguishes the Ashanikas tribe is their collective ferocious defence of their indigenous rights and territorial integrity. They can easily be called the "warrior-tribe" but I chose to name them "The Jaguar People" because of their readiness to defend their territory (as the jaguar does) and their facial ornamental adaptation of the jaguar-rosettes. At times of physical confrontation or protest against violators of their rights, the Ashanikas's jaguar-rosettes facial ornament serves to uplift their spirits and to help prepare them to face new challenges.

The Amazon Exploration Series   *Constantine Issighos*

The Jaguar People   *15*

The Amazon Exploration Series *Constantine Issighos*

The Jaguar People

The Amazon Exploration Series   *Constantine Issighos*

The Jaguar People

The Amazon Exploration Series   *Constantine Issighos*

The Jaguar People

The Amazon Exploration Series *Constantine Issighos*

The Jaguar People

www.ingramcontent.com/pod-product-compliance
Lightning Source LLC
Chambersburg PA
CBHW041755040426
42446CB00001B/39